WILDLIFE VIEWING AREAS

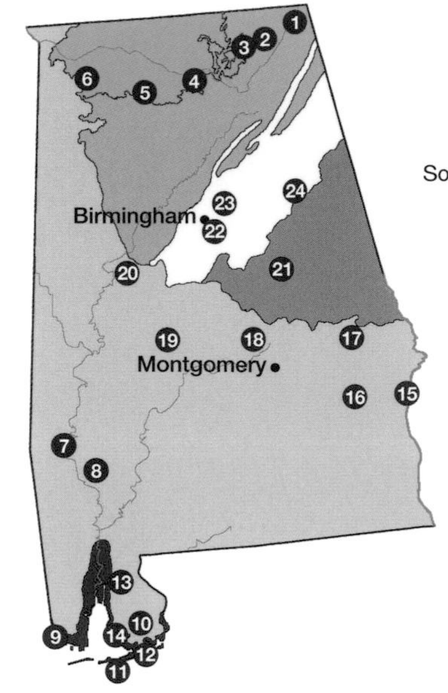

Alabama Ecoregions

- Southeastern Plains
- Southern Coastal Plain
- Southwestern Appalachians
- Interior Plateau
- Ridge and Valley
- Piedmont

1. Crow Creek Refuge
2. Sauta Cave National Wildlife Refuge
3. Fern Cave National Wildlife Refuge
4. Wheeler National Wildlife Refuge
5. Black Warrior Wildlife Management Area
6. Key Cave National Wildlife Refuge
7. Choctaw National Wildlife Refuge
8. Old St. Stephens Historical Park
9. Grand Bay National Wildlife Refuge
10. Biophilia Nature Center
11. Bon Secour National Wildlife Refuge
12. Gulf State Park Nature Center
13. Gatra Wehle Nature Center
14. Weeks Bay Interpretive Center
15. Eufaula National Wildlife Refuge
16. Robert G. Wehle Nature Center
17. Louise Kreher Forest Ecology Preserve
18. Alabama Nature Center
19. Perry Lakes Park
20. Alabama Museum of Natural History
21. Hollins Wildlife Management Area
22. McWane Science Center
23. Ruffner Mountain Nature Center
24. Anniston Museum of Natural History

Most illustrations show the adult male in breeding coloration. Colors and markings may be duller or absent during different seasons. The measurements denote the length of animals from nose/bill to tail tip. Butterfly measurements denote wingspan. Illustrations are not to scale.

Made in the USA

Waterford Press publishes reference guides that introduce readers to nature observation, outdoor recreation and survival skills. Product information is featured on the website: **www.waterfordpress.com**

Text & illustrations © 2011, 2023 Waterford Press Inc. All rights reserved. Photos © Shutterstock. Ecoregion map © The National Atlas of the United States.

To order or for information on custom published products please call 800-434-2555 or email orderdesk@waterfordpress.com. For permissions or to share comments email editor@waterfordpress.com.

ISBN 978-1-58355-671-9
$7.95 U.S.
50795
UPC 8 84682 00904 5
10 9 8 7 6 5 4 3 2 1
2301402

A POCKET NATURALIST® GUIDE

ALABAMA WILDLIFE

A Folding Pocket Guide to Familiar Animals

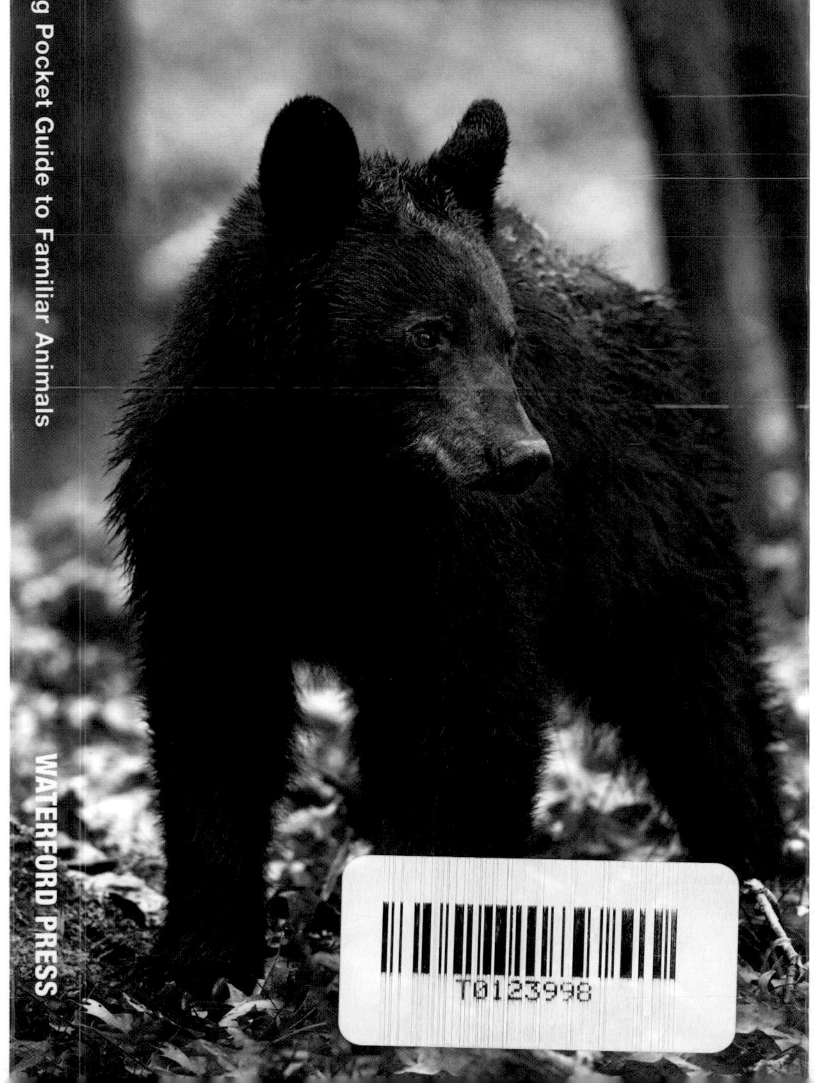

ALABAMA WILDLIFE – A Folding Pocket Guide to Familiar Animals

WATERFORD PRESS

T0123998

SEASHORE LIFE

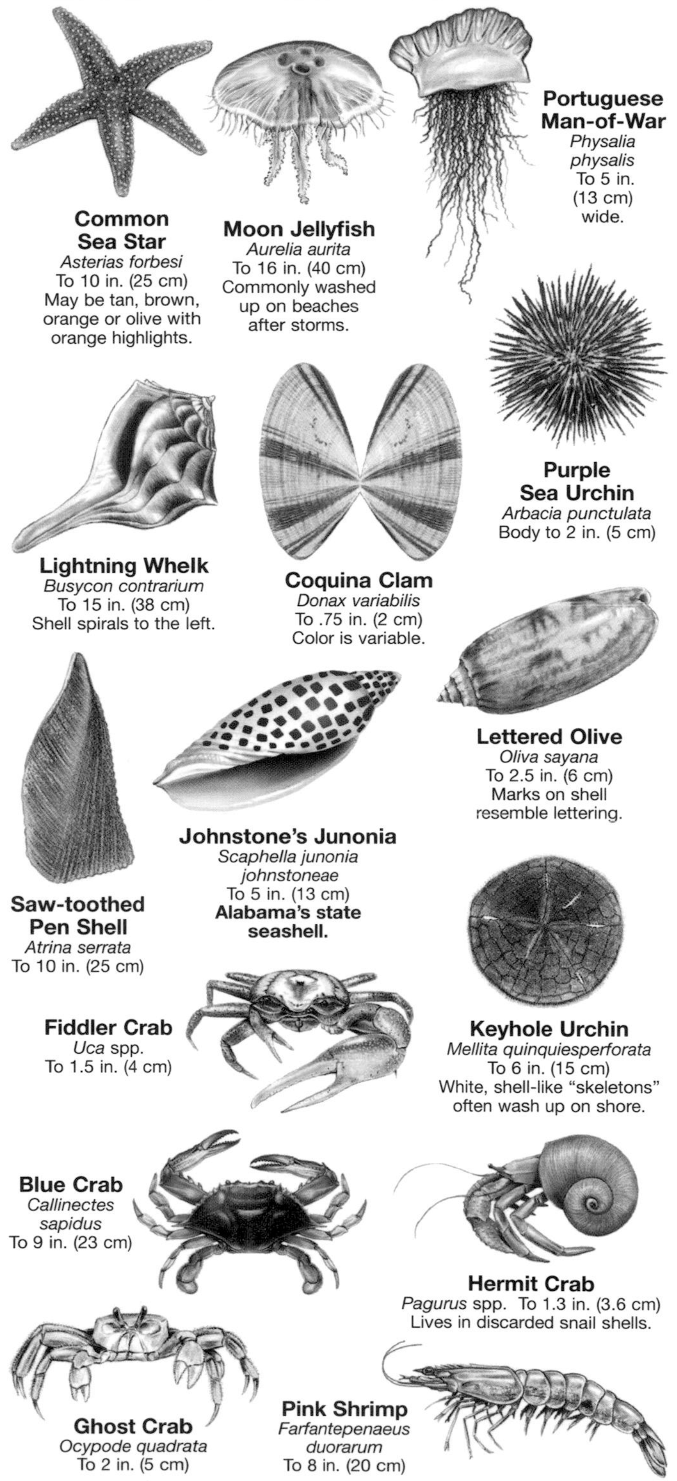

Common Sea Star
Asterias forbesi
To 10 in. (25 cm)
May be tan, brown, orange or olive with orange highlights.

Moon Jellyfish
Aurelia aurita
To 16 in. (40 cm)
Commonly washed up on beaches after storms.

Portuguese Man-of-War
Physalia physalis
To 5 in. (13 cm) wide.

Lightning Whelk
Busycon contrarium
To 15 in. (38 cm)
Shell spirals to the left.

Coquina Clam
Donax variabilis
To .75 in. (2 cm)
Color is variable.

Purple Sea Urchin
Arbacia punctulata
Body to 2 in. (5 cm)

Lettered Olive
Oliva sayana
To 2.5 in. (6 cm)
Marks on shell resemble lettering.

Johnstone's Junonia
Scaphella junonia johnstoneae
To 5 in. (13 cm)
Alabama's state seashell.

Saw-toothed Pen Shell
Atrina serrata
To 10 in. (25 cm)

Fiddler Crab
Uca spp.
To 1.5 in. (4 cm)

Keyhole Urchin
Mellita quinquiesperforata
To 6 in. (15 cm)
White, shell-like "skeletons" often wash up on shore.

Blue Crab
Callinectes sapidus
To 9 in. (23 cm)

Hermit Crab
Pagurus spp. To 1.3 in. (3.6 cm)
Lives in discarded snail shells.

Ghost Crab
Ocypode quadrata
To 2 in. (5 cm)

Pink Shrimp
Farfantepenaeus duorarum
To 8 in. (20 cm)

INVERTEBRATES

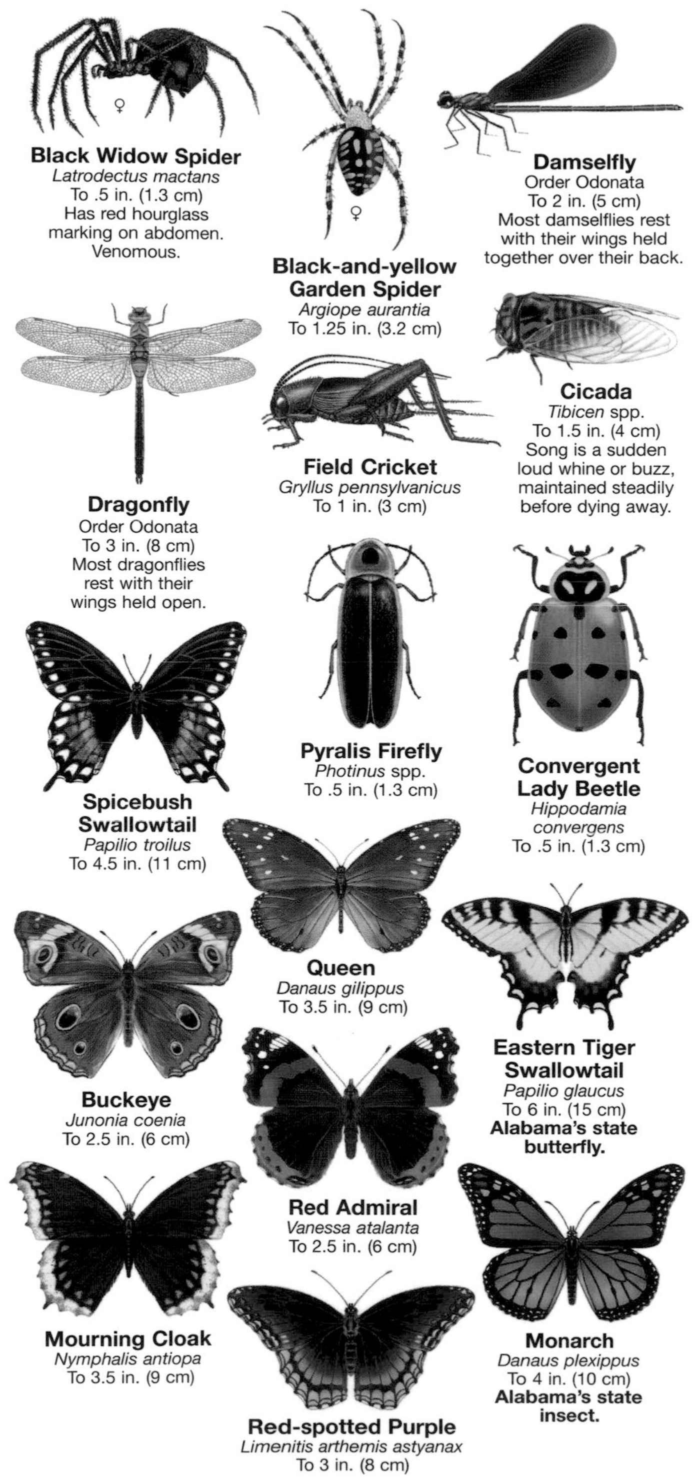

Black Widow Spider
Latrodectus mactans
To .5 in. (1.3 cm)
Has red hourglass marking on abdomen. Venomous.

Black-and-yellow Garden Spider
Argiope aurantia
To 1.25 in. (3.2 cm)

Damselfly
Order Odonata
To 2 in. (5 cm)
Most damselflies rest with their wings held together over their back.

Cicada
Tibicen spp.
To 1.5 in. (4 cm)
Song is a sudden loud whine or buzz, maintained steadily before dying away.

Field Cricket
Gryllus pennsylvanicus
To 1 in. (3 cm)

Dragonfly
Order Odonata
To 3 in. (8 cm)
Most dragonflies rest with their wings held open.

Pyralis Firefly
Photinus spp.
To .5 in. (1.3 cm)

Convergent Lady Beetle
Hippodamia convergens
To .5 in. (1.3 cm)

Spicebush Swallowtail
Papilio troilus
To 4.5 in. (11 cm)

Queen
Danaus gilippus
To 3.5 in. (9 cm)

Eastern Tiger Swallowtail
Papilio glaucus
To 6 in. (15 cm)
Alabama's state butterfly.

Buckeye
Junonia coenia
To 2.5 in. (6 cm)

Red Admiral
Vanessa atalanta
To 2.5 in. (6 cm)

Mourning Cloak
Nymphalis antiopa
To 3.5 in. (9 cm)

Red-spotted Purple
Limenitis arthemis astyanax
To 3 in. (8 cm)

Monarch
Danaus plexippus
To 4 in. (10 cm)
Alabama's state insect.

FISHES

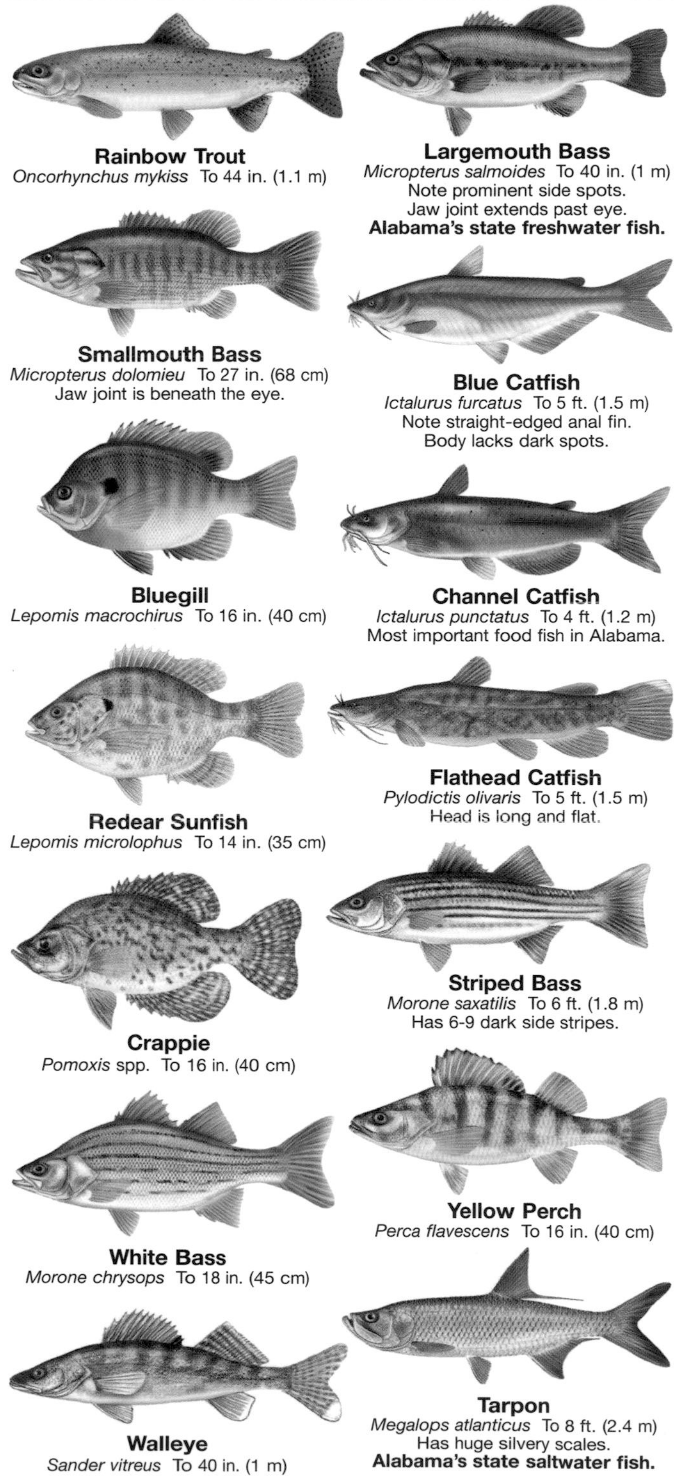

Rainbow Trout
Oncorhynchus mykiss To 44 in. (1.1 m)

Largemouth Bass
Micropterus salmoides To 40 in. (1 m)
Note prominent side spots. Jaw joint extends past eye.
Alabama's state freshwater fish.

Smallmouth Bass
Micropterus dolomieu To 27 in. (68 cm)
Jaw joint is beneath the eye.

Blue Catfish
Ictalurus furcatus To 5 ft. (1.5 m)
Note straight-edged anal fin. Body lacks dark spots.

Bluegill
Lepomis macrochirus To 16 in. (40 cm)

Channel Catfish
Ictalurus punctatus To 4 ft. (1.2 m)
Most important food fish in Alabama.

Redear Sunfish
Lepomis microlophus To 14 in. (35 cm)

Flathead Catfish
Pylodictis olivaris To 5 ft. (1.5 m)
Head is long and flat.

Crappie
Pomoxis spp. To 16 in. (40 cm)

Striped Bass
Morone saxatilis To 6 ft. (1.8 m)
Has 6-9 dark side stripes.

White Bass
Morone chrysops To 18 in. (45 cm)

Yellow Perch
Perca flavescens To 16 in. (40 cm)

Walleye
Sander vitreus To 40 in. (1 m)

Tarpon
Megalops atlanticus To 8 ft. (2.4 m)
Has huge silvery scales.
Alabama's state saltwater fish.

REPTILES & AMPHIBIANS

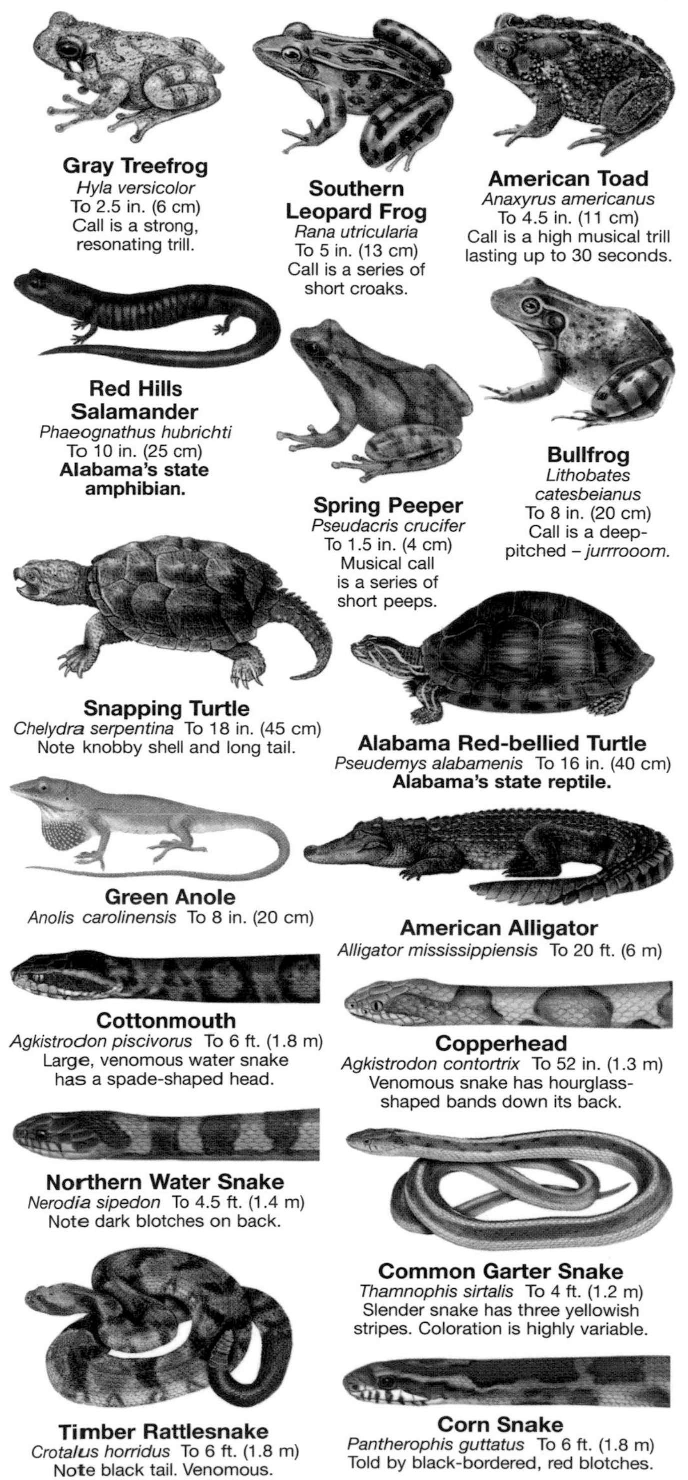

Gray Treefrog
Hyla versicolor
To 2.5 in. (6 cm)
Call is a strong, resonating trill.

Southern Leopard Frog
Rana utricularia
To 5 in. (13 cm)
Call is a series of short croaks.

American Toad
Anaxyrus americanus
To 4.5 in. (11 cm)
Call is a high musical trill lasting up to 30 seconds.

Red Hills Salamander
Phaeognathus hubrichti
To 10 in. (25 cm)
Alabama's state amphibian.

Spring Peeper
Pseudacris crucifer
To 1.5 in. (4 cm)
Musical call is a series of short peeps.

Bullfrog
Lithobates catesbeianus
To 8 in. (20 cm)
Call is a deep-pitched – *jurrrooom.*

Snapping Turtle
Chelydra serpentina To 18 in. (45 cm)
Note knobby shell and long tail.

Alabama Red-bellied Turtle
Pseudemys alabamenis To 16 in. (40 cm)
Alabama's state reptile.

Green Anole
Anolis carolinensis To 8 in. (20 cm)

American Alligator
Alligator mississippiensis To 20 ft. (6 m)

Cottonmouth
Agkistrodon piscivorus To 6 ft. (1.8 m)
Large, venomous water snake has a spade-shaped head.

Copperhead
Agkistrodon contortrix To 52 in. (1.3 m)
Venomous snake has hourglass-shaped bands down its back.

Northern Water Snake
Nerodia sipedon To 4.5 ft. (1.4 m)
Note dark blotches on back.

Common Garter Snake
Thamnophis sirtalis To 4 ft. (1.2 m)
Slender snake has three yellowish stripes. Coloration is highly variable.

Timber Rattlesnake
Crotalus horridus To 6 ft. (1.8 m)
Note black tail. Venomous.

Corn Snake
Pantherophis guttatus To 6 ft. (1.8 m)
Told by black-bordered, red blotches.

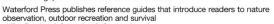

Mallard
Anas platyrhynchos To 28 in. (70 cm)

Wood Duck
Aix sponsa To 20 in. (50 cm)

Canada Goose
Branta canadensis
To 45 in. (1.14 m)

Black-crowned Night-Heron
Nycticorax nycticorax To 28 in. (70 cm)

Great Blue Heron
Ardea herodias
To 4.5 ft. (1.4 m)

Great Egret
Ardea alba
To 38 in. (95 cm)
Note yellow bill and black feet.

White Ibis
Eudocimus albus
To 28 in. (70 cm)
Juveniles are brownish.

Green Heron
Butorides virescens
To 22 in. (55 cm)

Snowy Egret
Egretta thula
To 26 in. (65 cm)
Note black bill and yellow feet.

Cattle Egret
Bubulcus ibis
To 20 in. (50 cm)

Ring-billed Gull
Larus delawarensis
To 20 in. (50 cm)
Bill has dark ring.

Black Skimmer
Rynchops niger
Feeds by skimming over water with its lower bill cutting the water's surface to spear fish.

Laughing Gull
Leucophaeus atricilla
To 18 in. (45 cm)

Double-crested Cormorant
Phalacrocorax auritus
To 3 ft. (90 cm)
Note orange-yellow throat patch.

Turkey Vulture
Cathartes aura
To 32 in. (80 cm)
Note red head.

Black Vulture
Coragyps atratus
To 27 in. (68 cm)
Note gray wing tips.

Red-tailed Hawk
Buteo jamaicensis
To 25 in. (63 cm)

Anhinga
Anhinga anhinga
To 3 ft. (90 cm)

Bald Eagle
Haliaeetus leucocephalus
To 40 in. (1 m)

Osprey
Pandion haliaetus
To 2 ft. (60 cm)

American Kestrel
Falco sparverius
To 12 in. (30 cm)

Barred Owl
Strix varia
To 2 ft. (60 cm)
Call is a loud –
who-cooks-for-you? who-cooks-for-you-all?

Great Horned Owl
Bubo virginianus
To 25 in. (63 cm)
Call is a resonant –
hoo-HOO-hoooo.

Belted Kingfisher
Megaceryle alcyon
To 14 in. (35 cm)

Ruby-throated Hummingbird
Archilochus colubris
To 3.5 in. (9 cm)

Northern Bobwhite
Colinus virginianus
To 12 in. (30 cm)

Mourning Dove
Zenaida macroura
To 13 in. (33 cm)
Call is a mournful –
ooah-woo-woo-woo.

Yellow-billed Cuckoo
Coccyzus americanus
To 14 in. (35 cm)

Barn Swallow
Hirundo rustica
To 8 in. (20 cm)
Note deeply forked tail.

Wild Turkey
Meleagris gallopavo
To 4 ft. (1.2 m)
Alabama's state game bird.

Yellowhammer
Colaptes auratus
To 13 in. (33 cm)
Wing and tail linings are yellow.
Also know as the Northern Flicker.
Alabama's state bird.

Pileated Woodpecker
Dryocopus pileatus
To 17 in. (43 cm)
Note large size.

Downy Woodpecker
Dryobates pubescens
To 6 in. (15 cm)
The similar hairy woodpecker is larger and has a longer bill.

Red-headed Woodpecker
Melanerpes erythrocephalus
To 10 in. (25 cm)

Purple Martin
Progne subis
To 8 in. (20 cm)

Carolina Wren
Thryothorus ludovicianus
To 6 in. (15 cm)
Note white eyebrow stripe and wing bars.

Carolina Chickadee
Poecile carolinensis
To 4.5 in. (11 cm)
Song is a name-saying –
chickadee-dee-dee.

Ruby-throated Hummingbird
Archilochus colubris
To 3.5 in. (9 cm)

American Crow
Corvus brachyrhynchos
To 22 in. (55 cm)
Call is a distinct – caw.

European Starling
Sturnus vulgaris
To 8 in. (20 cm)

White-breasted Nuthatch
Sitta carolinensis
To 6 in. (15 cm)

Red-winged Blackbird
Agelaius phoeniceus
To 9 in. (23 cm)
Song is a gurgling –
konk-la-reee –
followed by a trill.

Boat-tailed Grackle
Quiscalus major
To 16 in. (40 cm)
Long tail is keel-shaped.

Common Grackle
Quiscalus quiscula
To 14 in. (35 cm)

Eastern Bluebird
Sialia sialis
To 7 in. (18 cm)

Blue Jay
Cyanocitta cristata
To 14 in. (35 cm)

Gray Catbird
Dumetella carolinensis
To 9 in. (23 cm)
Repetitive call of variable sounds is interspersed with cat-like mew notes.

Northern Mockingbird
Mimus polyglottos
To 11 in. (28 cm)
When singing, it often mimics sounds around it. Many of the phrases are whistled, but it also makes sharp rasps, scolds and trills.

Brown Thrasher
Toxostoma rufum
To 12 in. (30 cm)

Yellow-rumped Warbler
Setophaga coronata
To 6 in. (15 cm)
Note yellow on rump and crown and white throat.

American Robin
Turdus migratorius
To 11 in. (28 cm)

Baltimore Oriole
Icterus galbula
To 8 in. (20 cm)

Common Yellowthroat
Geothlypis trichas
To 5 in. (13 cm)

Eastern Meadowlark
Sturnella magna
To 9 in. (23 cm)

Indigo Bunting
Passerina cyanea
To 6 in. (15 cm)

Northern Cardinal
Cardinalis cardinalis
To 9 in. (23 cm)

Dark-eyed Junco
Junco hyemalis
To 7 in. (18 cm)

American Goldfinch
Spinus tristis
To 5 in. (13 cm)

House Sparrow
Passer domesticus
To 6 in. (15 cm)

Eastern Towhee
Pipilo erythrophthalmus
To 9 in. (23 cm)
Cheerful song is – drink-your-tea or drink-tea.

House Finch
Haemorhous mexicanus
To 6 in. (15 cm)

Evening Grosbeak
Coccothraustes vespertinus
To 8 in. (20 cm)

Virginia Opossum
Didelphis virginiana
To 40 in. (1 m)
Note long fur and naked tail.

Eastern Chipmunk
Tamias striatus
To 12 in. (30 cm)
Note white stripes on side and face.

Eastern Cottontail
Sylvilagus floridanus
To 18 in. (45 cm)

Southern Flying Squirrel
Glaucomys volans
To 10 in. (25 cm)

Swamp Rabbit
Sylvilagus aquaticus
To 22 in. (55 cm)

Fox Squirrel
Sciurus niger
To 28 in. (70 cm)
Note large size and bushy tail. Coat may be dark gray, red-brown or black.

Eastern Red Bat
Lasiurus borealis
To 5 in. (13 cm)

Eastern Gray Squirrel
Sciurus carolinensis
To 20 in. (50 cm)

Northern River Otter
Lontra canadensis
To 52 in. (1.3 m)

White-footed Mouse
Peromyscus leucopus
To 8 in. (20 cm)
Distinguished by its white undersides and hairy tail.

Common Muskrat
Ondatra zibethicus
To 2 ft. (60 cm)
Aquatic rodent that has a naked tail that is flattened on its sides.

Woodchuck
Marmota monax
To 32 in. (80 cm)

Nine-banded Armadillo
Dasypus novemcinctus
To 32 in. (80 cm)

Mink
Neovison vison
To 28 in. (70 cm)
Chin is white.

Long-tailed Weasel
Mustela frenata
To 21 in. (53 cm)

American Beaver
Castor canadensis
To 4 ft. (1.2 m)

Common Raccoon
Procyon lotor
To 40 in. (1 m)

Striped Skunk
Mephitis mephitis
To 32 in. (80 cm)

Bobcat
Lynx rufus To 4 ft. (1.2 m)
Has dark lines on top of its "bobbed" tail.

Eastern Spotted Skunk
Spilogale putorius
To 22 in. (55 cm)

Black Bear
Ursus americanus
To 6 ft. (1.8 m)
Alabama's state mammal.

Common Gray Fox
Urocyon cinereoargenteus
To 3.5 ft. (1.1 m)
Note black-tipped tail.

Coyote
Canis latrans To 52 in. (1.3 m)

Red Fox
Vulpes vulpes To 40 in. (1 m)

White-tailed Deer
Odocoileus virginianus
To 7 ft. (2.1 m)
Fluffy tail is white below and held aloft when running.

Wild Hog
Sus scrofa
To 6 ft. (1.8 m)

Manatee
Trichechus manatus
To 11.5 ft. (3.5 m)